Joe Safdie's poems in *The Oregon Trail* exe
killed and eaten– and I like it that way. Here, eaters watch themselves get eaten. In this
there is a certain tenderness and sensuality. Safdie's poetry straddles death from every
direction, marks and transgresses its boundaries, and brings access in the living moment
to poetry's inherent formality, the pleasure it takes in itself. By lyric paths, in erudite
yet straight-forward poems, modes of being find material to play with. Orpheus and
Hermes are but two mythic faces that Safdie invents (invenies: I discover) along the high
bridge of a bird's flight between nothing and nothing, where they are still living, and
have not quite become themselves. The Oregon Trail of Safdie's lyric, through whatever
medium, unfolds. This is the trail of Gunslinger and The Loom—the trail that consumes
and leaves one with only a dubious and fleeting wisdom, for which any poet would
barter all their gold, and more.

   Tamas Panitz

Like a modern day sometimes vehicular flaneur, wandering among the ruins,
treasures, and bric-a-brac of our throwaway civilization, Joe Safdie brandishes his
considerable erudition in *The Oregon Trail* to focus on phenomena as they pass our line
of sight or flit through the mind, giving us another version of realism.

   Ammiel Alcalay

Poems from his retirement are evidence that a real poet never retires—
he just doesn't have to drive to work. In an *activa vita* retirement, Joe Safdie recognizes
two of his formative teachers. He names a section of the book "Hermes, the Thief,"
after Norman O. Brown's first book. And in another section, the scholar of Edward Dorn
and the Via Negativa writes: "[T]he only logical reading choice / in the time of the
coronavirus / is Cioran." I take my Cioran before long walks in Safdie.

   Richard Blevins

Out West along the Pacific coast poet Joe Safdie has retired from decades
of slogged academic doldrums & moved north from sunny San Diego to the far more
cloudy and wet urban chic yet green inlay of Portland, OR. Thankfully the power of his
poetry has only gathered momentum. His inter-textual dances have all the moves, just
like Lee Konitz and Peggy Stern discover in Lunasea. We're all grateful to have Safdie
keep on blowing.

   Patrick Dunagan

THE OREGON TRAIL

Joe Safdie

SPUYTEN DUYVIL
New York City

ACKNOWLEDGMENTS

The poems "(Untitled)," "Prophecy," "the theme music for *Succession*" and "Orpheus Again" appeared in *Typescript* (ed. Theresa Smalec); "Goodbye La Jolla" and "Joanne" were published in *Dispatches from the Poetry Wars* (ed. Michael Boughn and Kent Johnson); and "on the negative" and "Yachats OR" appeared, in slightly different versions, in *Blazing Stadium* (eds. Tamas Panitz, Whit Griffin, and Lila Dunlap). Deep thanks to the editors for their often unacknowledged but essential work.

The cover illustration is by Cary Meshul, one of my oldest friends, who also did the cover illustration for my first chapbook, *Wake Up the Panthers,* in 1974. More of his art can be seen at http://www.carymeshulart.com/

Thanks as well to my commentators and colleagues: Michael Boughn, Ammiel Alcalay, Richard Blevins, MT Cronin, Patrick Dunagan, Tamas Panitz, Robert Hogg, Catherine Tobin, and the other members of the post-*Dispatches* email group: you know who you are.

Library of Congress Cataloging-in-Publication Data

Names: Safdie, Joe, author.
Title: The Oregon trail / Joe Safdie.
Description: New York City : Spuyten Duyvil, [2021]
Identifiers: LCCN 2021024309 | ISBN 9781952419997 (paperback)
Subjects: LCGFT: Poetry.
Classification: LCC PS3569.A277 O74 2021 | DDC 811/.54--dc23
LC record available at https://lccn.loc.gov/2021024309

THE POEMS, AS ALWAYS, ARE FOR SARA.

THE OREGON TRAIL

AFTERWORD BY ROBERT HOGG

RETIREMENT

(Untitled)

imagine pulling the trigger
bodies crumpling and bursting
in front of your weapon
pure instinct now

eighteen more shot
if a few seconds later
the bullets pierce your armor
the rush of death

the twisted synapses
the seamless transaction
the endlessly repeated tweets
conferring legitimacy

the bestowal of blame
the strict poetic form

Prophecy

In the future humanity will be optional,
not available in all areas. Most of us
will be hooked up to machines,
with constant opportunities to offload.

There will still be people who are interested
in the arts, who drink wine and wear
interesting clothes, but they'll live
in out of the way places that don't

look the way we remembered them,
with different weather patterns.
The conversations will seem familiar,
but after we've been in one

we won't remember a thing about it.

Goodbye La Jolla
man on freeway
punching his cellphone
near stalled car
aggressive Mercedes drivers

whiz past at 85
gardening truck in the slow lane
languid pines drooping
in hazy sunshine

eucalyptus   slender   graceful
all the other trees
too snotty to change colors
the calm of the entitled

hoodies and sunglasses
in 70-degree weather

Directional
people say the west
    is the direction of death
probably because the sun and moon
       seem to die there

   (does the moon
      have a green flash too?)

likewise
      if you say you came from the east
   you wouldn't be far wrong

but then all those people who gather for sunsets
      really make up a death cult
not really seeing anything
   just looking back inside themselves

Joanne

so soon?
    I needed more instruction
        in the everyday
Cody lying luxuriously
    in the front yard
↑   belly up
light wind blowing across
    the sagging tree dahlias
you never had time
       for sadness

so we'll feel it for you
    vibrant one
        mocking one
    just space

February 2

Imbolc – "in the belly" – Lady Day,
candle light and ewe's milk,
"a holy day going back 5,000 years" –
sacred to Brigid, goddess of fire,
of poetry, and of healing –

creative powers of spring
buried under blankets
of snow and fog –
they're talking about replacing
the groundhog with an algorithm

February 9
I always look forward
to the *in memoriam* segment
of the Oscars
when the dead
for a brief moment
become more important than the living

the theme music for *Succession*
has "cemented its status in sonic TV history"
according to an article in *Vulture* –
I can testify to its weird zen chime/
orchestral combination, but the show,
a more fictional portrayal of Fox News
than *The Loudest Voice* on Showtime

and therefore subject to the usual
right-wing blather about persecution
from liberal elites, also has good writing –
"syphilis is the MySpace of STDs,"
for example, or a conference presentation
called "The Qualities of Inequality"

for the 1% of the 1%, or "you should try
swallowing something," a witty reminder
of a difficult biological feat detailed
in the season's first year, all of which
were probably inspired by Frank Rich,
one of the executive producers

(a sexual harassment complaint broken
by *New York* magazine on a cellphone) –
and great characters, especially "Shiv,"
the supremely sassy Murdoch daughter,
who's doubled as campaign advisor
for a lefty presidential candidate

but who might succeed her father,
unless betrayed, which happens often
(Brian Cox a good deal crazier
than Russell Crowe's Roger Ailes) –
her two brothers are good too,
the compulsive drug addict, who

would have noticed that homonym
and won an Emmy for it, and
the bratty young Trumpian punk,
working within the system
or blowing it all up on a whim –
did people ever debate using

pop culture in poems? Probably,
but while migrants are caged
at the border, the earth floods and burns,
a president is impeached
and people we love die or suffer
unaccountably it's amazing that

even under the rule of machines
and reduced to a data stream
(Vox acquires New York Media, now
owns *Vulture* and *New York* magazine)
we can still sometimes summon
a faint, endlessly conflicted smile

Orpheus Again
I smoke marijuana to return
        to the level of the stones –
or if not their splendid
   geological history
at least the surrounding
   shrubs and grasses
      dancing in place –

and that was the only secret
   to his music –
the real Orphics
   weren't so quick to imagine
      a way out of the world –
as the story has it
   this is it

for Norman Finkelstein

Retirement
nothing to do
old Sherlock Holmes movies
snowy new moon Pisces

the comforts of etymology:
re means "again" so this
isn't anything *new,* just

(remembering "attire")
different clothes, thick
sweaters, flannel shirts

for the "Great Northwest,"
refugees from SoCal sun –
the OED calls it "withdrawal

from the world or the society
of others" while *The Faerie Queene*
mentions "this safe retyre of life"

in opposition to the "vaine shadows"
that confront us in the world –
"the act of falling back,

retreating, or receding from a place
or position" – certainly what's
happening here, as teaching's

now confined to the screen,
privacy rights undisputed,
invisible, no longer part

of the favored demographic,
not catching anyone's eye –
"just cleaning things up

"so the invaders can come in"
wrote Spicer – long slow lesson
in learning to disappear.

I've made it to Innisfree
Uncle Will, clothing optional,
whether my body goes

underground or scatters
to the far winds or waves,
starting again, as if

none of the past years
had meant anything at all . . .
who goes with Fergus now?

*

the great Northwest
always had a bit
of an inferiority complex

beavers and ducks
on the Pac-12 Network
never quite the equal

of glitzy California
or sun burnt Arizona
this night the beavers

prevail over the ducks
but not those ducks
floating down the Willamette

temporary back yard view
reading Gary Snyder again
rivers and mountains without end

what makes a poem
"maximum fancy" said Nada
on her Facebook feed

but that was never it for me
being plain isn't great
but at least it's instinct

not paraphernalia
n'er so well expressed –
words don't capture

what I want anymore,
watching the river's
faint tides ebb and flow . . .

geese waddle out
in broken formation
I'll follow them tomorrow

          *

"I was really caught up at that time
in looking for the simplicity
what simplicity I could find

in the English language
and so I thought
well, pre-Norman English –

the Germanic lineage
of the English language –
has a lot of monosyllables

and monosyllables are like rocks
and I was used to working
with these rocks, and I thought

I'm gonna try to work
with monosyllabic English,
like I was building

a little rock trail"
I'm in pieces
bits and pieces

   *

looks like we won't see
total blood red eclipse –
skies too rain-soaked –

  blood red total eclipse
  total red blood eclipse
  red total blood eclipse

have to pay attention
to things closer to home
like *True Detective*

the main character haunted
by his ex-wife
at different times in their life,

alive and dead – he forgets
when he's old and also when young –
"don't go in for remembering stuff" –

links between everyday repression
and senility cyber technology
the war against memory

old and confused seniors
inability to get with the program
what the hell were you doing

why did you join the army
at the end of Mishima's tetralogy
the 80-year-old Buddhist nun

didn't remember her childhood friend
from the first volume   had no idea
of what he was talking about

what if the ending isn't
really the ending at all
what if there's another story

a premonition from an old lover
I have this condition
I forget things

      *

the titles of my two last poems have been
"Proclus on Place as the Luminous Vehicle"
and "True Detective 3" –

now the dental office waiting room
occasionally catching a glimpse
of people in offices through windows

of the building across the street –
the other window has a view
of other downtown Portland buildings

which I'll need to learn to identify,
many under construction, impassive
in grey skies, yellow cranes bifurcating

their verticality, like a Léger painting.
I subscribed to the *Times Literary Supplement*
three years after I heard Lydia Davis say

she was obsessed with it at a reading –
don't mind the lag, it's built-in.
Anyway, this Paul Muldoon poem

in the issue I brought along,
"American Standard," isn't bad:
the title is the brand name of a toilet.

It's big and digressive like many
of my own poems, juggling
lots of different themes.

Elsewhere in this issue I learned
that "ubermensch" doesn't mean
a really good guy but

Nietzsche's Superman – how did *he*
get in here? I'd recently liked
Muldoon's poem for Leonard Cohen

in a small volume of resistance poems
I picked up at my first visit
to my new local bookstore –

that's the thing about Portland:
lots of trees, pages, books . . .
I dream about teaching every night.

Hermes the Thief

remembering Norman O Brown

The recognition, the insight, the memory, the brilliant idea,
have this in common, that they come suddenly, as we say,
"into a man's head." Often he is conscious of no observation
or reasoning which has led up to them. But in that case,
how can we call them "his"?

   —*The Greeks and The Irrational* by E. R. Dodds

There were really five Mercuries

   —*Giordano Bruno and the Hermetic Tradition* by Frances A. Yates

poetry and magic
not the Spicer Circle
but the realm of Hermes
elusive   mercurial
kicking up chalk on the foul line

a dream address
everyone is there
already broken into groups
not chosen by lots
the lecture hadn't yet begun

if everything we see
is someone else's spell
sleight of hand
card tricks
when the world is the cards

Scholarly Dilemma
whether to dig up Karl Kerenyi's *Hermes*
from its taped-up box in the garage
or spend forty bucks on Amazon . . .

Ah!   Inter-library loan!

there was a third way of living life,
besides the Apollonian rational
and the Dionysian irrational . . .
Hermes' way, the way of "roguery"

God of jokes and journeys, thieves
and magicians, the tricky Guide of Souls

Hermes the only one that is going
to rob you or enrich you,
enlighten you or screw you.

the split-second timing
the spirit of finding and thieving
                —from *Hermes: Guide of Souls* by Karl Kerenyi
                                (Introduction by Charles Boer)

Hermes the revolutionary
the common man
"uncouth"   "rude"
Nobby's Marxist phase

independent in *The Iliad*
he only later became
the messenger of Zeus

along with the rise of kings
and the consequent expansion
of his cult

the Greek Hermes is the most versatile,
enigmatic, complex, and ambiguous.
The runt of the Olympic litter,
he is the god of lies and tricks,
yet is also kindly to mankind
and a bringer of luck;
his functions embrace both
the marking of boundaries
and their transgression . . .
he also plays the role of mediator
between all realms of human and divine activity,
embracing heaven, earth, and the Netherworld.
　　　　—from *Tracking Hermes, Pursuing Mercury*, ed. John F. Miller

Hermes has no need to fight for his center
he does not have one
　　　　—from *Hermes and His Children* by Rafael López-Pedraya

Oregon Coast, Late May
my older books
(*Saturn Return, September Song*)
    often explored
        demarcated stretches of time*

but now my muse is Hermes
    god of space-time
        offering Hermetic wisdom
while stifling a laugh

we must be moving on
    backwards or forwards
        not the relevant consideration

what takes place
    has no particular time

---

*As when this poem began, when a number of planets were in aspect to my natal Mercury – Jupiter and Mercury squaring it, Venus, Saturn and Pluto sextile, Neptune conjunct – and sadly, Gerrit Lansing wasn't around to explain any of it.

Mercury, Hermes, Thoth
invented the script, letters, palette;

the indicated flute or lyre-notes,
on papyrus or parchment

are magic, indelibly stamped
on the atmosphere somewhere,

forever (HD, "The Walls Will Not Fall")

to the accusation of theft
        Hermes would ask
    what is ownership

Hermes also commerce
        intersection of ideas
three forks in the road
   I was the cashier
      at my father's clothing store
seed is soul

        muse, sing Hermes
        the childish
        the petulant
          taking pleasure
            in misfortune
        the primitive
        the phallic
        the conniver
        the magician
        Autolycus
          with a god's quickness
        the secretive
        the scamp
        the musician
        pre-Olympian
          Titanic roots
            Atlas was his grandfather

He steals and hides Apollo's herd,
invents the lyre using strings made of cow's gut
stretched across a tortoise shell, and later
exchanges the instrument for Apollo's herd. . . . (Miller)

it's important that Hermes invented the lyre
because the poets
who sang the Iliad and the Odyssey
were playing it

Hermes gives his older brother
a music lesson, instructing Apollo
in the importance of a gentle caress
rather than a rough touch
that will make the instrument screech. (Miller)

but after teaching Apollo
more harmonious rhythms
he split

"god of the roads" also meant
roads that led out of Delphi

the erect phallus
a magic wand
to turn away harm

god of primitive trade
rituals at the boundary
let there be commerce between us

Hermes allows us
to receive messages
from gods and other strangers

translating foreign tongues
evading walls
buying and selling at the border

both this and that
neither this nor that
coyote   serpent

"deceitful" only
if wedded to a position
any position

the necessity of deception
in all human activity
therefore I lie with her and she with me

in constant revolt
against reigning dispensations
trickery means being alive

not stealing but revealing
all writers work in secret
and any secret action

is magic
a god of moments
he just moves

you can't get a fix on him
standing outside
the armed camps of the gods

Both Hermes' magical power to release
and the attendant power to bind
are illustrated by the so-called cursing tablets
inscribed with curses against persons named on them
and then buried in the ground

the Greek word for these tablets means "bindings"
and a number of them involve Hermes
as the one who holds down
or, as we say, the spellbinder . . .

Whereas Hermes was the master of words
throughout Greek culture, in the classical period
this meant primarily that he was the god of rhetoric

the earlier concept of Hermes as the master of word magic
persisted in the underworld of popular superstition
to rise again under the sign of Hermes Trismegistus
when popular superstitions became the dominant religious force
—from Hermes the Thief by Norman O. Brown (1947)

as to why so much scholarly material
I had a sheltered life
immersed in comic books and TV
until I met Professor Brown
and realized Greek myths
were the baseball box scores of the ancients

the *Homeric Hymn to Hermes*
was the Mueller report of the ancients
full of unpunished crimes
that nobody reads about
and so don't realize
are happening all the time

Hermes' presence in us enables us to feel
our own primitiveness, giving us a sense of instinct.
This is essential to any insight into Hermes:
an immediate sense of the reality of our being
      —from *Hermes and His Children* by Rafael López-Pedraya

the only way Hermes
might be thought of as heroic
is making possible
commerce between strangers

he's not going to save your soul
the phallus on the boundary stone
was just a good luck charm
for coming to an agreement

in primitive trade
the exchange in itself
is a ritual act

the paradox of his guiding and his leading astray,
the sudden giving and taking away,
the wisdom and cunning, the spirit of propitious love,
the witchery of twilight, the weirdness of night and death
—from *The Homeric Gods* by Walter F. Otto

the rules of plagiarism re-written
sacred thievery
knowing how to use what's stolen
sleight of hand

By the Willamette
in the classical conception
not even the nymphs
of wells and springs
live forever

primal waters
the arena of becoming
swamp and spring

Hermes followed memory
neh moh sen nay
making connections

others had forgotten
instinctual omens
psychic movement

slipping through keyholes
his sweet-talking very difficult
for Apollo to bear

Hermes, god
of crossed sticks,
crossed existence

Agh! brother spirit
what do they know
of whatever is the instant
cannot wait a minute
　　　　　　　—Robert Creeley, "Prayer to Hermes"

       muse sing Hermes
the inconstant one
    human on my faithless arm
the breaker of oaths
slipping free from bonds
sliding from commitment
    ashes floating
        the disappeared

squirrel clambering along telephone line
speedboat down the Willamette

astrology is the Trismegistus part
the psycho-pomp
the system maker

Hermes is the squirrel

The Three Sisters of Hermes
    are inspired
when they've fed on the golden honey
        and want to pronounce truths

If, however, they are kept away
      from this sweet food of the gods
then they try to lead you astray

the marvelous and mysterious
peculiar to night
may also appear by day
as a sudden darkening
or an enigmatic smile.
—from *The Homeric Gods* by Walter F. Otto

near the end of the Homeric Hymn
Hermes is promised
      a lesser divination skill by Apollo
he won't be able
      to discern the mind of Zeus
only the buzz and clatter
    and what he can make of it

the Padres game Sunday delayed
      by a cluster of buzzing bees
"the word for their swarming about
    means the swarming of the furious Maenads"

    Kerenyi is poetry in prose:
      "these enigmatic sisters are bees,
but as bees they are souls
    whose ability to prophesy
      depends on whether they are
full or empty – the Hermetic oracle
      is dependent on these conditions"

this is what we got
a swallow changes course
    cat lurks in the shadow
      of the deck chair

one more week on the Willamette

Twice in his wandering Ulysses is hopelessly stranded,
twice the narrative of The Odyssey starts faltering,
twice Hermes appears – to break Calypso's and Circe's magic –
in order to revitalize the narrative. Ulysses departs
and with him literature sets off again.
—from *Hermes: Literature, Science, Philosophy* by Michel Serres
(Introduction by Josue V. Harari & David F. Bell)

Hermes reveals himself
    when he goes before Zeus
        and lies
about stealing Apollo's cattle

Zeus roars with laughter
        "divine laughter
    that vouches for the harmlessness
        of the Titanic heritage"

a figure of astonishing ignorance and ineptitude
    has assumed power in the united states
different only in scale
    from those who preceded him

some people view this situation
        with outrage and alarm
    but only laughter
        can blow it to rags

> *then Lord Apollo, son of Zeus, said to Hermes:*
> *"Guide and Giver of Good Things, Hermes, Zeus' son,*
> *would you not care to lie in bed beside golden Aphrodite,*
> *even though you were snared by unbreakable chains?"*
> *The Messenger-God, Slayer of Argus, replied: "Lord Apollo,*
> *Far-Shooter, three times as many inescapable links*
> *could hold me, and you gods could be watching, and yes,*
> *all the goddesses too, if only I might sleep with golden Aphrodite."*
>
> *At this, laughter rose from the group of immortal gods. (The Odyssey VIII)*

"that the world of Hermes
     stands under a special sign –
that of deft guidance
          and sudden gain –
does not exhaust that world;

     to that world belong also
the rejected parts and the disavowed
     the phallic
          as well as the spiritual

the shameless as well
     as the gentle and merciful"
even if the connection between these qualities
          does not seem to make sense

     like Oppen's poetics
the poem exists
          before we put words to it
I started out
          with the materials to one side
     and then merged with them

One must therefore conceive of a philosophy
that would no longer be founded
on the classification and ordering
of concepts and disciplines,
but that would set out from an epistemology
of journey, forging new relations
between man and the world
                    —Michel Serres, *La Naissance de la physique*

Remember The Titans

in telling the stories of the Titans
it is better to follow Hesiod than Homer
who, like all his school of poets,
did not esteem tales of this sort
　　　　　　　—Karl Kerenyi, *The Gods of the Greeks*

saw *Jason and the Argonauts* at a Portland theater
and had NO IDEA that Zeus looked like that
(Honor Blackman, soon to be Pussy Galore,
triumphant as Hera) – Hermes described as
"a bringer of dreams and a prowler in the night" –

Jason didn't seem intimidated by the gods,
which seems right, as I read recently
that Graves' *Greek Myths* were made-up,
an unappreciated literary forgery –

Poseidon is what Aquaman should have been,
Talos the Titan had an Achilles heel,
the skeletons were scarier than White Walkers
and Medea as the love interest changed
the golden fleece into the royal scam –

the Olympians learned their violence
from the Titans – "let us continue
another day" said Zeus at the end –

I was the only one in the theater

Mercury Retrograde

let's go over it again
misunderstood communication
trouble conveying thoughts and intentions
mental obstacles

Mercury influences fast travel
and communication – when retrograde,
these aspects of life
can start feeling quite chaotic

flight delays; poor communication;
broken phones; car trouble;
computers crashing; lost packages;
chaotic emotions. "You might feel

Mercury retrograde is ruining your life,
but it's only doing so
for your greater good" –
issues that stop us in our tracks

also offer an opportunity to pause
and consider if what we're doing
is aligned with who we are
when Mercury goes retrograde   Hermes hides

Hermes is the father of eloquence, patron of orators,
musician, master of words, noise, and wind.
What does a parasite do? He takes and gives nothing
in exchange, or rather, gives words, noise, wind. . . .
Hermes: messenger, exchanger, parasite.
—from *Hermes: Literature, Science, Philosophy* by Michel Serres
(Introduction by Josue V. Harari & David F. Bell)

he becomes priapically aroused
through catching sight of a Goddess

the first evocation
        of the purely masculine principle
    through the feminine

the original Hermes
    had no special need
        of a love affair with Aphrodite
in order to beget Eros

        he possessed her
as his feminine aspect
    perhaps even the more prominent part

before the masculine nature in him
        became aroused

Hermes' Resumé
- helped Zeus cheat on Hera
- killed the hundred-eyed giant Argus (who was guarding Io,
  one of Zeus' girlfriends), lulling him to sleep with poetry
- took Dionysus to be raised by nymphs
- helped Orpheus take Eurydice from Hades
- told Paris to choose Aphrodite,
  causing the Trojan War (*see* hermaphrodite)
- gave Pandora her stealthy nature
- ordered Calypso to release Odysseus, gave him mole to resist Circe
- made sacred the ram, the hare, the crocus, the strawberry
- stole Ares from a brazen pot
- stole Hector's body from Achilles
- stole poetry from the Muses

cakes and smoked offerings
for Hecate
at the new moon

a kind of eroticism
one may find crass and vulgar
and a connection to souls and spirits
are characteristic for her

the Hermetic essence
seen in his most ancient
representations, may only to us
appear so low and vulgar

there it is precisely the crassest
that is the holiest & most spiritual

silver-white fluid metallic element, late 14c., from Medieval Latin *mercurius*,
from Latin Mercurius. Prepared in ancient times from cinnabar,
it was one of the seven metals (bodies terrestrial) known to the ancients,
coupled in astrology and alchemy with the seven known heavenly bodies.
Probably was associated with the planet for its mobility. Popular name: quicksilver.

From the Archives
the "Hermetic Tradition"
in Yates' Giordano Bruno book
    which I'd remembered as the borderline
        between John Dee and the Renaissance

turns out to be
    a quite late incarnation of Hermes,
        in which he loses all his sass

Victor Frankenstein too learned his science
    from Agrippa and Paracelsus
Mary Shelley so pissed off at Percy

that she had to navigate
    the transition from magic to science
        all over again

a deeply felt critique of Romanticism

Hermes' last trick in *The Iliad*
was spiriting Priam
behind enemy lines
to reclaim his son's body
giving humans a great gift

the full weight of their misery

Hermes the Thief: Epilogue
when the gods died
Hermes was taking a siesta,
his winged shoes on the pebbles

underneath the chaise –
it's true he caught something
on the wind, as they say,

but messages take work
and right now he just wanted
to lie back and sip a cold one –

nectar, of course – if he'd known
what life would be like
without that Olympian brand,

he might have flown up in alarm
and looked for a likely victim
to trick out of certainty,

but what would get through to us,
any hints of mythos muffled
behind our secular masques?

aspens quiver, reflecting
on the cell phone screen
as the signal goes out of range

Afterword

"Banquets do not always end in a foreseeable fashion.
One day, tomorrow, soon, one leaves life abruptly,
as one leaves the table – without having finished." (Serres)

I wish to thank my colleagues on this co-written adventure
through some of the winding ways of Hermes:

Hermes the Thief by Norman O. Brown (1947)

Giordano Bruno and the Hermetic Tradition by Frances A. Yates (1964)

The Homeric Hymns tr. Charles Boer (1970)

Hermes: Guide of Souls by Karl Kerényi (1976);
     "Preface to the 1995 Edition" by Charles Boer (1996)

Hermes: Literature, Science, Philosophy by Michel Serres;
     introduction, "Journal à plusieurs voies," by Josué V. Harari & David F. Bell (1982)

Hermes and His Children by Rafael López-Pedraya (1989)

The Eternal Hermes by Antoine Faivre (1995)

Tracking Hermes, Pursuing Mercury, ed. John F. Miller and Jenny Strauss Clay (2019)

And finally (courtesy of Patrick Pritchett), Hermes in the immortal *Jason and the Argonauts* (1963):
https://www.youtube.com/watch?v=XnxlF3Y2h4k

on the negative

THERE is in God (some say)
A deep, but dazzling darkness; As men here
Say it is late and dusky, because they
        See not all clear
O for that night! where I in him
Might live invisible and dim.
—Henry Vaughn, "The Night"

Once one has understood,
it would be best to drop dead on the spot.
What is to understand?
What we have really grasped
cannot be expressed in any way at all,
and cannot be transmitted to anyone else,
not even to oneself, so that we die without
knowing the exact nature of our own secret.
—E.M. Cioran, Drawn and Quartered

the only logical reading choice
    in the time of the coronavirus
        is Cioran

        ¤

    when meaning isn't clear
or deliberately obscured

      satire becomes available
    to ridicule that confusion

in that sense, it's rational
      often not even metaphorical

    the negative doesn't have
      an ideology

        ¤

the alchemists should have stopped with *nigredo*
    avoiding the ignominy and humiliation
        Of wanting more

        ¤

> *As I attempt to state the aporia of transcendence, I am caught in a linguistic regress. Each statement I make – positive or "negative" – reveals itself as in need of correction. The correcting statement must then itself be corrected . . . The authentic subject of discourse slips continually back beyond each effort to name it or even to deny its nameability. The regress is harnessed and becomes the guiding semantic force, the* dynamis, *of a new kind of language.*
> —Michael A. Sells, *Mystical Languages of Unsaying*

        ¤

the etymology of the word "apophatic"
apo phasis   un-saying or speaking-away
isn't necessarily *negative*
it just can't affirm anything

it's not talking to you

¤

Aleph is the first letter in the Hebrew alphabet. It has no pronunciation
in modern times, and if it indicates anything, it is the absence
of glottalization. I guess Greek would call it a smooth breathing.
Just an open. And as such, the most important of all letters has
no sound for them, and they derive tremendous cabalistic satisfaction
from this, a negative definition of God that can only define God
by what he is not or it is not. That privative definition of God is silence.
—Robert Kelley, "Threads 17"

¤

According to a Gnostic Revelation,
we fall short of the Most High
when we call Him infinite,
for He is, it is said, much more than that.
—Cioran, *Drawn and Quartered*

¤

For the optimist gnostic, matter is impregnated
with the divine, the earth lives, moves,
with a divine life, the stars are living divine animals,

the sun burns with a divine power,
there is no part of Nature which is not good,
for all are parts of God.

For the pessimist (or dualist) gnostic,
the material world heavily impregnated
with the fatal influence of the stars

is in itself evil; it must be escaped from
by an ascetic way of life which avoids
as much as possible all contact with matter . . .
 —Ficino, in *Giordano Bruno and the*
 Hermetic Tradition by Frances Yates

¤

magical thinking
 is suffering through hard times

  perhaps its severest demotion
since Descartes

¤

53

Negative: Webster's 1961

expressing   implying
or containing a negation
a *negative* answer
from *negare*   to deny

without affirmative statement
demonstration   character
a *negative* argument

not affirming the presence
of the organism in question
moving away
from a source of stimulation

denying a predicate
reckoned or proceeding oppositely
charged with negative electricity

¤

Comment on "Negative: Webster's 1961"

to deny
is an essential human function
people die every day
from the inability to say
"fuck you!"   although admittedly
fewer and fewer of us
lack this ability

¤

Garden Reading

       McLuhan's trivium on a good Friday
70 degrees in Portland
    almost unbelievable

"la culture chrétienne"
       fourfold exegesis
including allegory

but at least ancient grammar
    took the world into account
            and told stories about it

    unlike dialectics –
"the Cartesian revolution" –
       which assumed there was

some sort of truth
    at the end of logic
the other tree was different

    pre-lapsarian   *rerum natura*
       the world as a whole
variously inflected
       by the entities that compose it

    Adam in the garden, namin' names
       afterwards things got confused*

---

*The doctrine of names is, of course, the doctrine of essence and not a naïve notion of oral terminology. The scriptural exegetists will hold, as Francis Bacon held, that Adam possessed metaphorical knowledge in a very high degree. To him the whole of nature was a book which he could read with ease. He lost his ability to read this language of nature as a result of his fall; and Solomon alone of the sons of men has ever recovered the power to read the book of nature. (McLuhan)

¤

my latest thoughts on poetics
      are that the classical trivium
of grammar, dialectics and rhetoric

         (about which McLuhan
wrote his dissertation)
      pretty much describe poetry

first one feels the logos
            streaming across the heavens
the earth as one body

      then studies ways to express it
truth has nothing to do with it

"The great grammarians are, for reasons
to be made clear, also alchemists" (McLuhan)

                    ¤

The Tradition
paradiso in tercets
      (the companion is Virgil, not Ovid,
            for obvious reasons)

surviving through Renaissance romance
            and Giordano Bruno
      intensely mythopoeic

through Vico and Blake and Joyce
and McLuhan's doctoral thesis
      the stream of images . . .

there's also another way
      much flatter
            and a lot less Catholic

            ¤

Garden Reading 2

baseball cap and
　　The Figure of Beatrice
　　　　to protect from the sun

trying to recapture
　　the sense of a full universe
　　　　rerum natura　　four-fold

relief from the emptiness
　　of quarantine
　　　　isolato　　only my iPhone

knows I'm here
　　but negative theology
　　　　is still theology –

the Way of Rejection, "most familiar
　　　　in the records of sanctity" –
it's just not poetry

　　　　　　¤

It may be that Dante's Way – the Way of Images –
could not be too quickly shown to the world
in which the young Church lived.
It was necessary first
to establish the awful difference
between God and the world
before we could be permitted
to see the awful likeness
　　—Charles Williams, *The Figure of Beatrice*

　　　　　　¤

this small white butterfly
        fluttering along the lavender
    exists in itself

but also represents
        anxious motion
    everything we've had to forget

to exist is good
    but you also need
        to represent

> *Hell is the cessation of work and the leaving of the images to be,*
> *without any function, merely themselves* (Charles Williams)

it's not one and two
it's one *as* two
    one isn't enough
        two is too many

                        ¤

I first read Dionysius the Areopagite
    in the summer of 1975
        in an Athens library

I'd just graduated from UC Santa Cruz
        and had a bad case of crabs

> *nor can it be described by the reason or perceived by the understanding,*
> *since it is not number, or order, or greatness, or littleness*
> *and since it is not immovable nor in motion, or at rest, and has no power,*
> *and is not power or light, and does not live and is not life;*
> *nor is it darkness, nor is it light, or error, or truth,*
> *free from every limitation and beyond them all*

                        ¤

Cratylus wanted no part
　　　of Socratic logic-chopping –
even the speech in the dialogue named after him
　　　was invented –
　　　　　he wouldn't deign
to express himself in words

　　　　　　¤

　　　　　　　　　　The poet is no dynamic genius but a clerk and a copyist whose
　　　　　　　　　　power, like that of Melville's Bartleby, is only through negation.
　　　　　　　　　　　　　　　　　　　　　　—Peter Gizzi on Spicer

a lot of Gizzi's poems
are dialogues between
apophatic and kataphatic
in a Keatsian kind of way –

these poems share that project
but I never let
positive theology interfere

since I was never a spirit
and never quite left the earth
all I do is watch

　　　　　　¤

an interview on NPR:
　　　what's the source of the miracles in this book?
　　　　　is it Moses or something?

　　　　　　¤

Garden Reading 3
should I break the mood
of reading David Rattray
because the cretin is on TV?
I should not

¤

Garden Reading 4
I could have survived
the whine and hum of the saws
and the crashing of the limbs

but when "Hotel California"
    came on the AM
        it was time to go inside

¤

a dream, arguing against perfection
    (not a huge stretch)
three people around a coffee table
        one of whom was Joanne

the universities are closed
    where, she asked, is learning
        to take place?
(she was joking)

¤

three months earlier, a short story idea:
a young girl who's only known isolation
is forced to mingle –
"our country set a new record
for deaths today" (4-3-20)

¤

"follow the science"
    as if that will help
    the only way out is through

to realize how deep a shithole
    we've dug for ourselves

¤

is it wrong
    to spend the quarantine
watching a *Battlestar Galactica* marathon?

"if you feel empty when you pray
    to Zeus, or Aphrodite, or Poseidon
    it's because it is empty –

a totally empty experience – they're not real –
    they've been promulgated by a ruling elite
    to stop you from learning the truth"

¤

to *savor* cynicism
    like a good Chardonnay
    no dime-store despair allowed

¤

March Madness suddenly sane . . .
quiescent . . . comatose . . .
sports disappears . . . serotonin shortage . . .
panic sets in . . . no toilet paper . . .

> *Today progress and barbarism are so intertwined as mass culture*
> *that only barbaric asceticism against this latter . . . may again*
> *produce that which is un-barbaric. No work of art, no thought*
> *which does not innervate the rejection of false wealth . . .*
> *has a chance to survive.* —Adorno, *Minima Moralia*

the trouble with Adorno is that he uses words like "innervate"

> *Perspectives must be produced which set the world beside itself,*
> *alienated from itself, revealing its cracks and fissures, as needy and*
> *distorted as it will one day lay there in the messianic light . . . It is the*
> *simplest of all things, because the condition irrefutably calls for such*
> *cognitions, indeed because completed negativity, once it comes fully into*
> *view, shoots [zusammenschiest] into the mirror-writing of its opposite.*

¤

drawing from the well
of emptiness
inexhaustible

¤

The Invisible Enemy

I'm trying to imagine
how fast it goes –
as fast as light?
As those clouds across the sky?
As the dark shadow
I caught a glimpse of in Oaxaca
when I looked up from my laptop
in early February?
I thought that was death
putting me on notice
but it had a larger audience
in mind, to be everyone's
enemy, killing by what's
known but not seen,
the sensitive spots –
"Harmony invisible
over visible prevailing"
wrote Heraclitus –
earth out of balance –
the clouds rain down
their terrible death upon us

¤

Heraclitus was a pretty smart guy
so he should have figured out
a better way to die
than to drown in cow shit

¤

These ghostly subatomic particles
stream from the Big Bang, the sun,
exploding stars and other
cosmic catastrophes, flooding the universe
and slipping through walls and our bodies
by the billions every second,
like moonlight through a screen door.
  —Dennis Overbye, "Out There," *NYT*

¤

The event horizon occludes the interior. There is no fact about the interior
of the black hole that can possibly be transmitted to the outside universe
because the event horizon forbids the transmission of any information or
any facts about the interior. The actual matter of the star becomes irrelevant,
except for the impression left behind in the form of the event horizon.
Shed the impression of the black hole as a dense crush of matter.
Accept the black hole as a bare event horizon, a curved empty spacetime,
a sparse vacuity, a glorious void, an empty venue, an extreme, spare stage . . .

This is what you must remember:

The black hole event horizon is empty.

The black hole is no thing. The black hole is nothing.

—Janna Levin, *The Black Hole Survival Guide*

¤

everything locked down
      no freedom of movement
  or thought
     the need for surveillance
of the virus

      and its carriers
line up for your gold star

      ¤

the horror of being carried along by senselessness,
by the movement of sluggish mentalities,
easily diverted by commodity culture
and by the allure of the erotics of the urban scene . . .
it is not a conscious strategy "to make strange,"
as in surrealism or other experimental modes . . . it is
more clearly a response, a "shock defense" as he calls it,
where everything is made strange by circumstance
      —Michael Heller on Benjamin

      ¤

I always thought of myself
as a scavenger   even as a kid
I mouthed other's words,
predicting what they were going to say
and why I use so many quotes
is because I can still hear them

      ¤

Among the Quarantined
marijuana smoke swirling
momentarily encased
in beam of sunlight
through office window
does it change the words
is there a world in this one

                         *

a neighbor's tree obscures
the view of Mt. Hood
outside my living room window
while Robert Mitchum pursues
the young daughter of Gregory Peck
"I saw that man – he chased me"
mangroves of south Florida
pines of Portland
the confined life of the privileged
distractions on every screen
"the structure of capitalist dream time
is most fragile"

                         *

interior design
at Zoom readings –
how the books are arranged
in back of the speaker
"like a man teetering
on the brink of his abysses,
tempted equally by the rushing current of objects
and by the whirlpool of self"
the two uppermost thoughts
in a Man's mind
are the two poles of his World

                    ¤

a constructed constellation of disparate moments
or perspectives . . . a disturbance in the "smooth" trans-
mission of historical happening under capitalist dream
time. The image encapsulates not a "present"
but a "now," "loaded to the bursting point with time."
         —Max Pensky on Benjamin

                      ¤

Benjamin's now-time
or Bonnefoy's "The Present Hour"
which at worst is recycled Stevens
but also offers a prayer for poetry
(not that it deserves it)

                     are you going to think
         That there is being only in images but that this
         Suffices as mystery, inasmuch as
         This nothingness consents to the light –
         Indifferent, uncreated – by the gestures
         Of it contours, its shifts, of the laughter
         In the depths of its tragic voice carrying
         Towards others some of these shadows. Perhaps not.

my preference is much for the last two words
but at least it's an open question

       ¤

the poetics of 1915
the poetics of 1959
inspiration, sure
then comes the exhale

     . ¤

hope isn't optimism, wrote Havel,
not grounded in the possibility
that everything will turn out well
its horizon is beyond the actual

"history says don't hope
on this side of the grave"
Heaney's character agrees
"but then, once in a lifetime,

the longed-for tidal wave of justice
can rise up, and hope and history rhyme"
nice work if you can get it

back in central Europe,
Havel's countryman Kafka
said there was "plenty of hope,
an infinite amount of hope –

but not for us"
i.e., it's not a plot that ends happily
it's not even a plot

¤

Reunion
saw two ex-students
   at the AWP
       something I said
     might have helped them
sustain their goals
    bad pedagogy
the only people who should hope
     are characters

        ¤

This year we should celebrate not only our birthdays,
but the birthdays of all those denied more birthdays by a
combination of natural causes and unnatural governance.
—Ryan Matthews

      ¤

The National Human Genome Research Institute
   (whose maps once seemed
      portals of immortality)

   describes viruses as existing
"near the boundary
     between the living and the nonliving" –

we invite them in –
   we're the hosts

        ¤

In this crisis of my fate I learned, as a lawyer
and a student of history and of economics,
to look on man, in the light of evidence
of unnumbered centuries, as a pure automaton,
who is moved along the paths of least resistance
by forces over which he has no control.
In short, I reverted to the pure Calvinistic philosophy.
As I perceived that the strongest of human passions
are fear and greed, I inferred that so much and no more
might be expected from a pure democracy
as might be expected from any automaton so actuated.
        —Brooks Adams

                                        ¤

Modern melancholics, despite their posturing,
nevertheless retain at bottom
a sort of fatuous optimism.
In contrast, the "organized pessimism"
of surrealist practice takes as its first goal
the violent, laughing expulsion
of all moral metaphors from politics
        —Max Pensky, *Melancholy Dialectics*

                                        ¤

the apophatic detectives
are on the case
24/7   and the world
is everything that is the case

        ¤

Henry VIII was a tyrant, and that increased his popularity.
There is hardly anything a human being can do to arouse more enthu-
siasm and universal acclaim than to become a successful tyrant, for
tyranny has a distinction of its own – especially when the tyrant is jovial,
hearty, and on the common level; and not a cultured, dignified person
philosophizing in a marble palace.
　　—W. E. Woodward, *A New American History*

¤

the truth is that humans are just a brief algorithm
　　　　—*Westworld*

¤

defensive pessimists are destroyers of worlds, but it is,
for the calamity-howlers, constructive – far more useful
than trying to cheer up. There is no cheering up,
as far as defensive pessimists are concerned . . .

you know this time could be different. You start picturing all the things
that could go wrong. What if I
spill coffee on the interviewer? What if I accidentally
deliver the presentation in a foreign language?
What if I forget my own name? . . .

The depressives almost always figured out
when they had no control. The non-depressed
had a much harder time. A significant number of them
cheerfully assumed they had agency . . .
　　　　—Jennifer Senior, *New York Times*

¤

Holidays
I'm going to start mailing packages from Amazon
with nothing inside them
"What's at the door from Amazon?"
"Nothing!"

¤

(the following quotes from *Mystical Languages of Unsaying* by Michael A. Sells)

(A Family Dispute)
kataphatic theology affirms the divine in positive language,
while the apophatic statement says the deity must be considered
beyond goodness   beyond being   beyond wisdom   beyond life

a battle between "the Great Chain of Being" and its inversion,
without structured hierarchy or thrones (Pound's Cantos) –

a pattern of procession and return,
the emanation out from the deity
and the eventual return of all things

Tashlich
you can use pebbles
instead of bread crumbs

in fact, you can just pretend
you're throwing something away

(The Idolatry of the Preposition)
Locked within seemingly innocuous words like "in," "to," "into,"
"from," and "before" is a semantic delimitation, a circumscribing
of the unlimited within spatial and temporal categories . . .
to believe such spatial connotations can be willed away is to
become all the more vulnerable to the "monstrous and abomina-
ble idols" hidden within such language . . . Are these spatial and
temporal metaphors not simply a tortured way of speaking?

Where Are My Poems
forgot to bring my poems to the reading
crossed off the list   null set
nothing rehearsed   nothing to say
creation from nothing
the cloud of unknowing   *agnosia*

3 October
reviewed some Islamic material
          and remembered that Sufis
     track back to the Suras
when Mohammad visits heaven
     with the angel Gabriel –
          reading Ib'n RushD
     in the apophatic book –
the trouble is that earth is heaven
     "strictly speaking
          there is no dualism here"
the thirty birds are the 30 Birds
the secular as spiritual
     as a spirit needs
          "Think stone" (Charles Stein)

two years into Portland
winter still brings dread
the odd Japanese maple
in the back yard
the only living thing
to retain color (red)
amidst the grey drizzle

(The Attraction of Submission)

encirclement is the movement of one object around another object –
that second object exists before it is encircled

in the emanation metaphor, however,
the things that are encircled are the result of the encircling

insofar as they are within
the gnostic power that enriches them,
they are the power that encircles them

Back When Philosophy Mattered
John Donne was worried about
the breaking of the chain
"now new philosophy calls all in doubt"
nothing in its proper place
death everywhere
no possibility of redemption

(The Last Quotation)

For everything that is understood and sensed is nothing other
than the apparition of the non-apparent,
the manifestation of the hidden, the affirmation of the negated

and the other things which cannot be retained
within the recesses of memory
and which escape the blade of the mind

> *negative people communicate better,*
> *think more clearly, make fewer mistakes,*
> *are less gullible, better at decision-making.*
> *The reason? Negative people have enhanced*
> *"information-processing strategies"*
> *which means they use the critical part of their brain*
> *more successfully than cheerful people.*
> *Negative people pay more attention to their surroundings.*
> *—James Adonis, The Sydney Morning Herald*

¤

I accept my inadequacy
my dis-equilibrium

there is no "first person"
 rumble of the freeway
  beyond the pines

¤

> *the dialectical image is the switch point*
> *where one point of view opens to another –*
> *where the monad is prized open by a diverging series. . . .*
> *"the point where plus becomes minus" . . .*
> *Then there is a leap into something else.*
> *—Miriam Nichols, Radical Affections*

¤

Garden Reading 5

the sun in Portland is so rare
that it seems petty to complain
about the morning chill
not having quite burned off

before noon, "at once advancing
and tarrying, a strange mixture of both"
Arendt was talking about Benjamin
in the quiet backyard garden:

For the Jews of that generation
the available forms of rebellion
were Zionism and Communism . . .

At the time Benjamin tried, first,
a half-hearted Zionism and then
a no less half-hearted Communism . . .

What mattered to him in both instances
was the "negative" factor
of criticism of existing conditions,

a way out of bourgeois illusions and untruthfulness,
a position outside the literary
as well as the academic establishment

¤

Tract

See! the hearse leads —Williams

from the Latin *tractus*
a tract of land,
drawing, track, from *trahere*
to draw (now poetic)

sorry for distracting you
it wasn't my intention
I'd like to retract
that statement   or maybe

just see distraction as
the opposite of "traction"
without sense of purpose
or point of motion

not strictly bound   abstract
an expanse   open-ended
with nothing to grasp
set adrift but not

just that   to detract
from a sterling reputation
I'd prefer not to
even consider the notion

I withdraw my consent
nothing more to grasp
this is an area
not subject to contract

¤

people who militate
      to get back to normal
   deserve what they get

     ¤

downfall
the descent beckons
wrote the doctor
down beat

     ¤

long thin jet streak
   momentarily obscures the sun

relatively few people have died
      here in the Great Northwest
   but they say the peak
      is still ahead

Afterword

The genesis of "on the negative" is in a paper I delivered in February 2020 at the Louisville Conference on Literature and Culture entitled "Edward Dorn, Satire, and the Via Negativa"; that paper was published in *Dispatches from the Poetry Wars* and can also be found on the website academia.edu. Among many others, I'd like to thank George Quasha for his recommendation of *Mystical Languages of Unsaying* by Michael A. Sells. As for the title, I'm not crazy about it, but *Journal of the Plague Year* was already taken.

Wagon Wheel at Big Bear (photo by Catherine Tobin)

Yachats OR

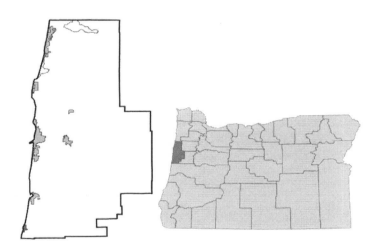

10-16-20
two hundred years to the day
since Byron began
Canto V of *Don Juan*

renting a house by the sea
in Yachats (rhymes with *les chats*)
we brought our cat

and together
    watch the receding tide

re-reading Kelly's *The Loom**
for inspiration
and John Dee MacDonald

        the Great Art
                of improvisation

"those seashore / moments when we know / we *are* at a shore & it *is* / a betweenland"

                    ↓

the name comes from the Siletz language
"dark water at the foot of the mountain"
at the 2010 census, the city's population was 690

                    ↓

10-19

Mon   day   after   noon
I'm just beginning to see
Juan in a Turkish harem

Kelly hanging
with Ramon Lull
and the Lady Isabella

on the way to Majorca
Travis McGee in Oaxaca
tracking down lost young

American crack heads
and receiving erotic instruction
from Lady Rebecca

> In her evident maturity, she was still totally girl, that special kind of girl who
> does not have any self-conscious awareness of herself, but can fling herself about,
> leggy and lithe, laugh with an open throat, comb her casual hair back with splayed fin-
> gers, scratch herself, kick off her sandals, stand ugly, lick crumbs from her fingertips.
> She was teeming and burning with endless and remarkable energies, with taut slender
> vibrating health. One could not imagine her ever being bored . . .

or so it was possible to write in 1969
(MacDonald, *Dress Her in Indigo*)
just a few years before *The Loom*
with its pantheon of goddesses

> I knew that all I had to work with was my body. I had to keep it as enticing as possible,
> because one must arouse intense desire, or the game is lost before it is begun, what? .
> . . I have absolute and independent control now of every muscle in my body, even all
> those reactions that are supposed to be involuntary responses to erotic stimulus. And
> all this time, my dear, I was studying all the books on the arts of love that I could find.
> Hindu, Arabic, Ancient Egyptian. I am now a repository of all that learning and skill.

Or as an article about the philosopher Martha Nussbaum posited:

> [she argued that] some forms of sexual objectification can be both
> ineradicable and wonderful . . . there are circumstances in which being
> treated as a sex object, a "mysterious thing-like presence," can be human-
> izing rather than morally harmful. It allows us to achieve a state that her
> writing often elevates: the "abnegation of self-containment and self-suffi-
> ciency." (Rachel Aviv, *The New Yorker*)

↓

in Canto V of *Don Juan*
Juan undertakes
a Dionysian transformation
dressed as a woman
in a Turkish harem

Baba eyed Juan, and said, "Be so good
    As dress yourself –" and pointed out a suit
In which a Princess with great pleasure would
    Array her limbs; but Juan standing mute,
As not being in a masquerading mood,
    Gave it a slight kick with his Christian foot;
And when the old negro told him to "Get ready,"
Replied, "Old gentleman, I'm not a lady."

"What you may be, I neither know nor care,"
    Said Baba; "but pray do as I desire:
I have no more time nor many words to spare." . . .

Before they enter'd, Baba paused to hint
    To Juan some slight lessons as his guide:
"If you could just contrive," he said, "to stint
    That somewhat manly majesty of stride,
T'would be as well and – (though there's not much in 't)
    To swing a little less from side to side,
Which has at times an aspect of the oddest –
And also could you look a little modest,

'Twould be convenient" (Canto V, LXXIII-IV, XCI-XCII)

as in *The Loom*
"All the pronouns
live in me"
when the male
becomes female & the female
male, & we move
naked at last
beyond the garments
male & female one
& none

that's the gospel of Thomas
which I read early on   1973 or so
right around the time
The Loom was being written
and which now manifests

as putting one's pronouns
at the end of e-mails
(Alice Notley's latest book
a new language with ones)
and while the inscription

"for my lady Helen"
seems a little dated
it's also sincere   in that
early 70s tone of voice
which couldn't help being

a little confessional
while absolutely serious
about alchemical fucking
            I can not explain –
            it will not

be Two & not
be None
but One
will not dance
alone.

As in a useful essay called "Reading *The Loom*" by Billie Chernicoff:

> Through his encounters with the anima, the Hero is at last delivered
> from himself into pure form, into change itself. He is at one with his labors.
> Time and space, music and matter, are one. Just so for the poet.

so process *is* content
the Great Art of Improvisation

> The duty was flesh
> & just to be there.
> He felt the music
> & was content with it.

Chernicoff also mentions *cantefable*: "spoken prose narratives interspersed with short songs"

In those days, the archetype "man" was without question heterosexual, physically
strong and muscular, sexually dominant, unemotional, stoic and non-communicative,
and committed to the hierarchal power of the status quo. However, . . . female power
helped erode the once-mythologized and real power of the hyper-masculine male. One
consequence is that the 21st century male is "sensitive," emotional, multi-sexual and
questioning of the status quo . . . the traditional link between patriarchy and hyper-
masculinity has come to be represented by blue-collar or working-class men, repre-
sented by construction and factory employees, fireman and policemen, "working class
men who take orders or lack status in other ways . . . resort to hypermasculinity in an
attempt to regain social status." (D. Rosen, *Counterpunch*)

Yachats sits at the base of the Oregon Coast Range along the Pacific 44° 18′ 40″ N, 124° 6′ 17″ W ¤ home to hiking trails at gorgeous Cape Perpetua Scenic Area, the highest point of the Oregon Coast ¤ attractions include sea lions at Strawberry Hill, Devil's Churn, and the best fish-and-chips stand on the Pacific Coast (Lunasea), commemorated in a Lee Konitz album of 1992

Cape Perpetua, near Yachats (photo by the author)

Deleuze fits in here too
"smooth space" like the sea
another formula
wedding stasis and motion
process and content
body and mind
i.e., it is what it is   until it isn't

& we move
in whatever way occurs to us
or opens to us
& the way itself
has meaning
only from the goal thereof.

↓

Of course, imitation — even of oneself —
is anathema to the pure, blank-slate invention
Mr. Jarrett still claims as his method.
"I don't have an idea of what I'm going to play,
any time before a concert," he said.
"If I have a musical idea, I say no to it." (Nate Chinen, *NYT*)

↓

The president and his followers are so very strong and manly that they can make
the liberals lose control of their emotions in the most helpless, ineffectual way. The
liberals are babies, maybe, or even worse – feminine. To be made to cry is not about
losing or paying, it is about humiliating. It is about strong people humiliating the
people they see as weak, for the fun of it, because they can. (*Washington Post*)

↓

my wife was snoring softly
in the moments before waking
it sounded like this

pain   pain   pain   pain
I don't want to get on that big black train
sings Lucinda   I believe it

↓

Neither the United States nor Great Britain had established sovereignty over the Pacific Northwest. Both countries wanted it and had some sort of claim, as did the Russians and the Spanish. But Lewis and Clark were the first white men to enter present Idaho, Washington, and Oregon by land. Although they never planted a flag to make a formal claim on the territory for the United States, they acted as if it were already theirs. (Stephen F. Ambrose, *Undaunted Courage)*

↯

[S]ome of the Louisianans were upset that women were competing for men's jobs and that the federal government "wasn't on the side of men being manly." Some male Kentucky interviewees, especially those who have a family history in coal, feel even more strongly that men's rightful place in the world is slipping away. Men in this community . . . "are starved for a sense of heroism. They don't feel good about themselves. They feel like they haven't done as well as their fathers, that they're on a downward slope . . . Their source of heroism, of status, is humming; it's fragile"

Her subjects think they can handle the virus just like Trump handles everything. "He's a two-hamburger-a-meal guy," she said. "He's kind of a bad boy, and they relate to that." [t]he president "comes off as a man. He doesn't come off as weak". . .

Mr. Trump channels "old-fashioned machismo" – "aggressive, physically tough, physically strong, never back down" – while Mr. Biden models "a more complex 21st-century version of masculinity," defined by "compassion and empathy and care and a personal narrative of loss." . . . "The era of the 'Pajama Boy' is over," Sebastian Gorka gushed in December 2016. "The alpha males are back." (Susan Faludi)

↯

the Clatsops and Chinooks . . . were thriving tribes before the smallpox hit them, still vibrant when Lewis and Clark came to spend the winter. . . . They loved the food and the climate, had perfectly adjusted to them, and rightly thought of the Pacific Northwest as a bountiful provider, almost paradise. To the captains and the men, it was a miserable place that they couldn't wait to get out of. (Ambrose*)*

↯

Blank Document

I'm trying out the font "Athelas" in this piece
even though I'm sure it's another modern knock-off
and not something steeped in printing history
(I'll have to look it up on *Wikipedia*)
because it sounds vaguely mythological
and I did want to touch on those matters

as Jupiter and Saturn are
closer together in the skies
than they've been in 500 years
and on the Winter Solstice
will in effect form a double star
religious people will think of Jesus

but pagans know otherwise,
Birth of Venus my screen saver
born from the foam of the severed penis
cut off by Kronos the avenging son
with the sharp teeth of Gaia's sickle
"the excised manhood of Father Ouranos

fell into the restless sea, into which
Kronos had cast it from the firm earth"
"and since the bloody deed of Kronos
the sky has no longer approached the earth
for nightly mating"   and people think *Trump*
was destructive   so this week he re-unites

with his son Jupiter (switching now
(to Roman terminology)   both squaring Venus
in my astrological chart   but tonight
December 9 is probably the clearest sky
we'll have in Portland for two weeks
so I'll interrupt the poem at this point

and see if I can see them   as they are now
a degree apart in late Capricorn

[line left blank in honor of experience
and poetry's absurd quest to capture the real
and the hope that negative space is generative]

reading now from du Beauvoir's *Second Sex*
where she quotes Byron from *Don Juan* (!)
"Man's love is of man's life a thing apart;
'Tis woman's whole existence"   which now
I'll have to find to cite   ('tho *she* didn't)
a passage whose sexism I at first rejected

but find that du Beauvoir agrees completely
with Byron about the slavish surrender
that love is for women   and which Kelly
in *The Loom* and Chernicoff's essay is at pains
to demystify   I don't know the story
of his separation from Helen soon afterwards

but she infuses the poem as her forebearer did
Homer's essentially masculine world
brought to a 19th century gloss by Byron
and that's what *Yachats* is about
that and the survival of Greek mythology
into 21st century poetry and poetics

meanwhile, what do you think of Athelas?
Regular   *Italic*   **Bold**   ***Bold Italic***
I was right it's an Adobe font
created in the historic year 2008
"inspired by British fine book printing"
"included as a system font in Apple's

macOS operating system"   in other words
about as far from mythology as you can get
"named after a healing herb
in Tolkien's *Lord of the Rings*"   hey
some people don't even *have* a history
and now to return to Venus on her shell

Wynd's *Pagan Mysteries in the Renaissance*
at hand   and of course Kelly's *The Loom*
its awkward early seventies vernacular
at times disguising its spiritual quest
the narrator a seeker of good poetics
(i.e. starting the poem with its typeface)

whatever lies at hand   an e-mail from Kent
comes through about his latest post
he told me that one of my recent poems
had the most surprising ending since Rilke's
"You must change your life"
(doesn't that make you want to read it?)

so I'll read his post but first listen
to Van Morrison's *Poetic Champions Compose*
which might be a theme of this poem
it turns out Botticelli's *Birth of Venus*
was a commission job   one Pierfrancesco
cousin of Lorenzo the Magnificent

and student of Ficino and Politian
too bad those appellations went out of style
I'd like to call my friends (on occasion)
"Magnificent" or "Ludicrous"   or both
as in many of Kent's posts and poems
the first cut "Spanish Steps" was instrumental

and totally fabulous   "Morrison follows his muse
wherever he likes. And every time, those
who have committed themselves to the journey
have been rewarded"   (*Rolling Stone,* 1987)
the album before this one was called
No Guru, No Method, No Teacher

and the lyrics to the second cut "The Mystery"
include "I saw the light of ancient Greece
Towards the One / I saw us standing
within reach of the sun"   except in Portland
of course   where the sight last night
of golden Saturn above and to the left

of brilliant Jupiter will have to be
the last I see with unaided sight
"There's a dream where the contents are visible
Where the poetic champions compose"
sings Van   almost as inscrutable
as Edgar Wynd writing about Venus

I think it has something to do with
Kantorowicz and *The King's Two Bodies*
mortality and its discontents
but Venus is always there
just about to step off the shell
and explode in your heart forever

even when you think it's not shattered
shards and fragments come from nowhere
(*especially* nowhere)   fierce stabs
at the heart for the love not given
and parents and grandparents finally
don't have much to say about that

What are the overlooked changes
that have emerged from technology?
"The technology that's seeping into every industry
has the capacity to do what the manufacturing sector
once did: help lift more people into the middle class.
A negative change is a tendency to trust

technology too much. Diagnostic software
in medicine is useful but also risky
if we rely on it without thinking. The ultimate
Hollywood example of dystopian tech is *Wall-E* (?)
technology making everything so easy
that we lose our personal agency"   there are probably

better examples than that in the middle class
six years from Carr's *The Glass Cage* and counting
campaign to convince people to take the vaccine
rural Americans tell science to fuck off   "COVID=HOAX"
the name of a Hearts player on my phone app   polio redux
disinformation on the internet by Robert Kennedy

luckily the sun and Mercury trine my Venus on Saturday
bringing back memories of the *Homeric Hymn to Hermes*
and providing relief from the Zeus-Kronos Square
breaking news: the clouds might part tonight (12-17)
to see Zeus inch ever closer   laying in wait
preparing the poison   ultimate momma's boy

his brothers and sisters swallowed
(common enough in the middle class)
Goya's tremendous painting
"the great Kronos   the tortuous thinker"
that out of this sexual violence love would arise
is a myth that needs further inspection

"That's a wrap on TechfestNW 2020 –
Portland's signature event that celebrates
the entrepreneur in all of us. This year
due to COVID-19, TFNW had to pivot
their originally planned in-person event
to a virtual platform"   Google & Facebook

under fire from the Feds   like Microsoft was
back in the nineties   you remember Microsoft
feared economic monopolist   (lots of chatter
about *Citizen Kane* this month with *Manc*
perhaps its greatest contribution to cinema)
now all they have left is Word

which I'm *not* knocking by the way
I've always found it more useful
than Pages or other programs I've tried
and it's certainly just as good as Adobe
who made the font I'm using in 2008
inspired by British fine book printing

like the cantos of *Don Juan* when they appeared
serially   close to when Byron wrote them
spontaneity a model then as now
Keith Jarrett in the background
there were people who thought
(and probably still do) that he wasn't important

not on the same level as Miles or Coltrane
I'll tell you in a minute once I listen
first I had to hear "If This is Goodbye"
from Mark Knopfler and Emmylou Harris again
the occasion some stanzas back for
intense emotional regret at lost love

which turns out to be Knopfler's tribute
for the victims of 9/11!   see, there's a place
for criticism   and the best critics
like Northrop Frye
are hanging with Blake
in a portal of the sky

an ad for iPhone 12 Pro Max deals
at the top of my Facebook ads
makes me momentarily forget
recent full-page ads in the *New York Times*
where Facebook excoriates Apple
one hysterically ending "StandUpForSmall"

"Great Kronos devoured all his children as soon as
each of them had left its mother's sacred womb . . .
he did not wish any other god to succeed
to his possession of this dignity"
"the great Kronos   the tortuous thinker"
the Golden Age in his belly   he threw it up

after being fed peyote by Jupiter
which led to all the other Ages
pandemics wars endless violence
some say the conjunction will end all that
but Jupiter has moved on   past the castrator
what was that about the Christmas star?

New Year Poem (Epilogue)
Byron had already finished Canto V
by November 20 1820
and here it is the end of the year already
a lot of people celebrating
but as a *Counterpunch* headline said
       "It Could Always Get Worse"

(why isn't that phrase seen
       as liberation?)
this poem started on the *TLS*
in some of the only white space available
    a poem by Ange Mlinko
       while watching *Star Trek: Discovery*

pop culture references
   middle to low brow
not many images
     and no similes like
"Like chimneys rising from an incandescence"
   (the first line of Mlinko's poem)

"How do we get Discovery to the future?"
   as good a question as any
like when poetic champions compose
     and under what planetary alignments
my wife doesn't like sci fi
   "how is it an intelligent guy like you . . ."

well, this episode   like *King Lear*
        queries whether forgiveness
                is possible (I usually tear up
when he recognizes Cordelia)
and questions skeptically
        our capacity to start anew

"to understand time we must
        disengage him from human logic"
poetry used to do that
                "you want me to just pick up
as if nothing happened?
                You have no idea."

and the limits of AI as well!
what is high brow
        the end of 2020
                a space odyssey
        ten days at the coast where time stopped
before starting over again

AFTERWORD
by Robert Hogg

Joe Safdie's *The Oregon Trail* is a collection filled with cold-eyed perception, deep affection for family and country, and a witty response to the challenges of language and scholarship as these impinge on his life and poetics. For those familiar with Parkman's original, the title will immediately hint that this venture will be mythic and historical, but it is much more nuanced. This is a poetry as loose and unstructured as the American saga that gave rise to both the original tale and to this contemporary venture; at the same time, it is intent on getting to the darker truths of our current condition large and small – and without pretense, though with a deal and a half of erudition.

Safdie's parameters are laid out in blocks of quoted material, often from texts on myth and early Greek culture from such stalwarts as Norman O Brown (with whom he studied earlier in CA), Karl Kerenyi, Walter F. Otto and others who have written cogently on the psychology and history of the Greek gods. One main focus is on an old friend, Hermes, so naturally I'm on side – but I wouldn't be if he missed the mark or put on airs in his performance: if anything, it's Safdie's reticence to pretend to knowledge that makes his work sing for me; his approach is rough and ready, flounders about at times, quotes perhaps too much for comfort—but so what, things fall into place, and the poem holds! Why? Because his project is genuine. As much as he incorporates history and myth, his poems are down to earth and about his daily life in Oregon where he now lives. Hermes does not feel like an invention, but is his natural angel, trickster, mercurial touch-stone. This is the Hermes we find in Hesiod's *Theogony* and in Charles Boer's energetic translation of the Homeric Hymns: stealer of cattle, creator of Apollo's lyre. But behind all this playfulness, what finally holds the poems together is Safdie's willingness to face a world of exceptional negativity, and to live *in* that negative space (hello John Keats), and never falsify it for the sake of a fine phrase, or for eloquence. There is plenty of jazz rhythm in his poetry too, but it does not occlude the subject which informs the poetry. Safdie's poems unflinchingly face up to a politically and a philosophically dark experience – the underbelly of America. That takes honesty and guts and creates a poetry you can believe in – even if it's explicitly NOT intended to offer any hope. It's a poetry that holds your nose to the millstone of reality, and you're not going to miss the smell of brimstone when it permeates the air – though his wit makes it tolerable, even fun. What is this? A *Comedia*?

With Joe's poem "Yachats OR," a title that completely flummoxed me before I figured out WHERE rather than what it cd mean, there are ways to locate oneself in the somewhat scattered writing. He does not set his reader at ease, but rather jerks him around on a kind of tether of his own making, yanking us this way, that way, by making unexpected statements of his own in conjunction with quotes from all manner of sources which provide a kind of map which also tethers us – his multiple real estate listings, so to speak--to provide us with 'homes' where we touch base and find ourselves, and the poet, in a common space together. His method may seem random, but I'm convinced it's not. And in this poem, at least, there is a geography which he constantly comes back to, particularly the area between the coast and Portland, OR. Like Pound and Olson, Safdie wants "a poem containing history" (and geography), and a whole lot of what's currently going on in his world. The poet is the chief locus of his poem, and it doesn't matter how wide the parameters get so long as he can rein them in to his cosmos, which he does, admirably. I had to do a pile of auxiliary reading to catch on to who was saying what, but it all feels worth it. Safdie doesn't *introduce* new ideas to his reader; he drops them in our lap, holus bolus, and lets us put them into context.

Deleuze fits in here too
"smooth space" like the sea
another formula
wedding stasis and motion
process and content
body and mind i.e.,

> **it is what it is until it isn't**
> > **& we move in whatever way**
> > **occurs to us or opens to us**
> > & the way itself has meaning
> > only from the goal thereof

I've emphasized a portion of the above passage because it expresses, baldly, Safdie's essential statement on his poetics, how he transmutes what he encounters, world or text, to discover meaning. What he does is *reveal*, not programmatically, but in an ad hoc manner, what he's taking in. If anything, the method is proprioceptive, a taking in of whatever presents itself to be ingested, even if it's more than he can chew! A kind of Romance with the whole world. A few lines beyond his reference to Deleuze, he writes, as though the two were intimately connected, the following:

> my wife was snoring softly
> in the moments before waking
> it sounded like this
> *pain   pain   pain   pain*

And then we're on a 'black train' and we realize this is the kind of headache you hear and can't get away from--and that you share. Here, Safdie breaks the sacrosanct rule of every MFA class: "Don't say the word "pain" if you expect your reader to feel it--it never works!" Well, I beg to differ. It sure as hell works here! Safdie breaks the rules. Both poem and reader benefit.

Sara Safdie

JOE SAFDIE's trail to Oregon included pit stops in California (San Diego, Bolinas, San Francisco, Venice Beach), Colorado (Boulder), Washington (Seattle) and the Czech Republic (Olomouc and Prague): now in Portland, he's studying the language of trees. Previous books and their publishers include *Mary Shelley's Surfboard* (Kevin Opstedal, Blue Press, 2008), *Scholarship* (Geoffrey Gatza, BlazeVox, 2014) and *Coastal Zone* (Tod Thilleman, Spuyten Duyvil, 2016).

Made in the USA
Las Vegas, NV
21 June 2021